The Death Penalty Debate

Exploring the Hidden Costs of Capital Punishment

Liam Wall

Copyright © 2016 Liam Wall

All rights reserved.

ISBN: 153039371X
ISBN-13: 978-1530393718

DEDICATION

To my Granddad for always inspiring me to write

CONTENTS

1 Introduction 1

2 A Brief Overview 3

3 Human Error 9

4 Deterrence 16

5 Morality 23

6 Closure 34

7 The Cost 41

8 Ultimate Justice 49

9 Conclusion 50

Books, offers, and more at

liamwallbooks.com

1 INTRODUCTION

For millennia, Capital Punishment has been exercised as a form of judicial discipline. Most countries have abolished this practice, but it is still prevalent in the United States of America, allegedly the most advanced democracy in the world.

The debate over the death penalty is one of contradicting studies, political agendas, and sometimes, plain ignorance. This issue is immensely complex and often impossible to understand.

In this book I have simplified the arguments of both sides down to three main points each.

Anti-Death Penalty:

1. Human Error

2. Morality

3. The Cost

Pro-Death Penalty:

1. Deterrence

2. Closure

3. Ultimate Justice

For too long, the death penalty has been in the shadows, and the government has, literally, been getting away with murder.

It's time to learn the truth about the death penalty.

2 A BRIEF OVERVIEW

Early History

In the United States, the death penalty has been around since colonial times. The first recorded execution haven taken place in Jamestown, Virginia, 1608. Captain George Kendall was executed by firing squad for spying for the Spanish government.

Public hanging became popular in the 1600s and continued throughout most of the 1700s as well. Newspapers at the time described these hangings as "festive events" but "always followed by violence."

The 19th Century

During the 19th century, there was a large movement to abolish the death penalty. This was a result of the "Jacksonian Era," which condemned the use of gallows and demanded more humane treatment of criminals.

Because of this movement, state penitentiaries were built, and the number of capital crimes was also reduced to only first-degree murder.

But this movement didn't last long, and opposition of the death penalty dwindled during the Civil War as a result of the conflict.

The 20th Century

During the first half of the 20th century there was a lot of progress made against the death penalty. Between 1907 and 1917, six states had abolished it. But, once again, this opposition was short-lived. When World War I began, supporters of the death penalty started to increase.

By 1920, five of the six states that had abolished the death penalty reinstated it.

The 21st Century

There are currently 31 states that support the death penalty, and 19 states that have abolished it.

States that support the death penalty include:

Alabama

The Death Penalty Debate

Arizona

Arkansas

California

Colorado

Delaware

Florida

Georgia

Idaho

Indiana

Kansas

Kentucky

Louisiana

Mississippi

Missouri

Montana

Nevada

New Hampshire

North Carolina

Ohio

Oklahoma

Oregon

Pennsylvania

South Carolina

South Dakota

Tennessee

Texas

Utah

Virginia

Washington

Wyoming

The death penalty is also endorsed by:

The U.S. government

The U.S. military

States that have abolished the death penalty include (Year abolished in parentheses):

Alaska (1957)

Connecticut (2012)

Hawaii (1957)

Illinois (2011)

Iowa (1965)

Maine (1887)

Maryland (2013)

Massachusetts (1984)

Michigan (1846)

Minnesota (1911)

Nebraska* (2015)

New Jersey (2007)

New Mexico** (2009)

New York (2007)

North Dakota (1973)

Rhode Island (1984)

Vermont (1964)

West Virginia (1965)

Wisconsin (1853)

and the District of Columbia (1981)

* In May 2015, Nebraska voted to abolish the death penalty. The status of the 10 inmates on death row is uncertain at this time. A petition has been submitted to suspend the repeal and put it to a voter referendum.

** In March 2009, New Mexico voted to abolish the death penalty. However, the repeal was not retroactive, leaving two people on the state's death row.

Suspended

In Furman v. Georgia (1972), the Supreme Court ruled that the death penalty was "cruel and unusual" punishment and in violation of the Eighth Amendment. The Supreme Court voided 40 death penalty laws. However, since not *all* laws were voided, the Supreme Court gave each individual state the option of making new laws for themselves, and many of the death penalty states took advantage of this.

Reinstated

Executions resumed with the execution of Gary Gilmore by firing squad on January 17, 1977 in Utah.

Lethal injection was adopted by Oklahoma as their primary method that same year, and all other death penalty states quickly followed suit.

Worldwide

All democracies around the world have abolished the death penalty, with the exceptions of the U.S. and Japan. The U.S. is the 5th largest contributor to the number of worldwide executions, despite this, the number of executions in the U.S. is dropping, with only 28 executions in 2015, down from 98 in 1999.

3 HUMAN ERROR

No matter how developed a justice system is, mistakes will always be made, but when it comes to the death penalty, these mistakes cost people their lives. The United States has a well-developed history of prejudice and bias in the courtroom. The system is broken, racist, and random, throwing out death penalties to whoever cannot defend themselves.

It is a lottery that no one wants to win.

And when the system is this random, you will always have innocent people on death row. Unfortunately, the numbers are larger than you would expect.

Innocent people on Death row

According to a new study, four percent of those given the death penalty are actually innocent.

This is a "conservative estimate," according to the researchers, who also pointed out that four percent is more than double the amount of exonerations from death row during the three decades that were studied.

This means that innocent people are unjustly losing their lives to the death penalty.

According to Samuel Gross, lead author of the study, and a University of Michigan Law School Professor, "The majority of innocent people who are sentenced to death are never identified and freed."

The study reviewed over 7,482 death sentences, spanning from 1973 to 2004. Only 117, or 1.6%, were exonerated.

The study also states that one of the leading reasons that innocent people are not exonerated is because they win appeals, reducing their sentence to life in prison. After this, the case is not pursued with the same vigor and they are left to rot in a cell.

The authors found that from 1973 to 2004, more than 35% of death row inmates had their sentences reduced. The authors concluded that if all cases were pursued like capital cases, the number of exonerations would surge. However, even by those calculations, we will never be able to free all of those who are wrongly convicted.

Mistakes Are The Norm

Many believe in the U.S. justice system, but it is important to recognize that it is not perfect. Even a few death penalty supporters admit that the process, like everything, is vulnerable to mistakes. But what people don't realize is that mistakes are not exceptions when it comes to the death penalty, but the norm.

Another study by researchers at Columbia University looked into 5,800 capital cases and found serious errors in 68% of them.

The researchers said that the death penalty is "collapsing under the weight of its own mistakes

There are also serious doubts in the minds of the researchers about the appeals process. They wonder how many of these errors appeals can catch, and how many of the appeals had errors as well.

The story of the death penalty is littered with examples of unjust trials, such as the one of Gary Graham. Graham was convicted on the testimony of just one witness, and lawyer, Ronald Mock, provided virtually no defense for Graham.

At the time of the trial, Mock already had five clients executed on his record, and 6 more on death row. Mock's clients were waiting for the adequate defense they were promised from the justice system. But they wouldn't get it, at least not from Mock, the lawyer that was assigned to them.

The government had given them the winning lottery ticket.

The lead author of the study from Colombia University, James Liebman, said, "All of the states are having more errors that they're generating than they're having success, and that's causing a real risk that something is going to go very badly wrong."

Clearly there is something wrong with the justice system as a whole, and the errors and risks increase exponentially when capital punishment is involved.

A Textbook Example

There are many examples of how this system is crippled. A perfect one is a case involving two North Carolina men, finally exonerated after 30 years on death row.

In September 1983, Sabrina Buie, an 11 year-old girl, was found murdered in North Carolina. She had been raped, beaten, and suffocated with her own underwear.

Within days the police had forced confessions from two teenagers, Henery Lee McCollum, 19, and his half-brother, Leon Brown, 15. They were both were convicted and sentenced to death.

Now, 30 years later, a state judge ordered their release after multiple pieces of new evidence proved their innocence. DNA taken from the crime scene matched a different man, Roscoe Artis, who was already serving a life sentence for a similar crime that took place just weeks after Sabrin Buie's murder.

In fact, Artis had been a suspect from the start. A few days before the trial of the two boys, police requested a fingerprint test to see if Artis matched a fingerprint found at the crime scene. The request was never completed, and this information was never given to the defense.

In 2011, the North Carolina Innocence Inquiry Commission discovered the request. They also found multiple statements in the forced confessions from the boys that were inconsistent with each other, and the crime. The Commission also matched the original DNA to Artis.

McCollum and Brown's lives are ruined. The system was rigged against them with all of the official errors and misconduct, making it harder and harder for them to have a fair trial. The whole case against them was built on *no* physical evidence, only the forced confessions given by the boys after hours of interrogation without a parent or lawyer present. If this doesn't prove that the death penalty system is flawed, how many more ruined lives will it take?

Back in 1984, the prosecution couldn't have cared less about the fact that the boys were innocent. The lead prosecutor was Joe Freeman Britt, dubbed as the "deadliest prosecutor" by the Guinness Book of World Records. During the span of his career, he was responsible for nearly 50 death sentences, almost all of which have been overturned because those convicted were found innocent.

These cases are distressingly common, and the death penalty is obviously unreliable with its flimsy evidence, and its bias.

Racist and Random

After the reinstatement of the death penalty in 1976, another study was published examining the trials of more than 2,000 homicides in Georgia, from 1972 to 1976. The study would become to be known as the Baldus Study, named after the lead author, and it found that black men were 1.7 times more likely to recieve the death penalty than any other race. They also found that convicts were 4.3 times more likely to recieve the death penalty for murdering a white person than if they had murdered a black person.

This racism is still prevalent nationwide. Since 1976, over 80% of those executed have murdered white victims. The Baldus study has also been repeated in states all over the U.S and the findings having always the same.

In Texas, 2008, district attorney Church Rosenthal resigned after news broke out that he had sent and received racist emails about his cases.

Rosenthal had sought the death penalty in 25 cases; his successor sought it in 7. Of these 32 cases, 29 of the defendants were black.

Out of all the states, Texas carries out the most executions. Since 1976, the state has executed more than 470 people.

Can you guess how many executions of a white man that murdered a black man there were?

One.

That's 0.002% of the total executions.

Our justice system is run under the assumption that you're 'innocent until proven guilty.' This should reflect our choice, as a society, to let some guilty people go free, rather than have innocent lives perish.

Is it too much to ask that we stop and pause for a moment to make sure that we are not killing innocent people?

Justice Potter Stewart once said that the death penalty is arbitrary, like being struck by lightning.

It still is… but when will society stop throwing the bolts?

4 DETERRENCE

What does the death penalty cause? We can say for sure it causes pain, it causes a loss of money, and it causes gridlocks in our court system. But does it cause the deterrence of murder? Many death penalty supporters say it does.

The logic behind death penalty deterrence is simple; capital punishment is worse than any other punishment in our justice system, so if we use it and criminals are afraid of it, it will lead to fewer killings. Optimistic pro-death penalty studies estimate that 3 to 18 deaths are deterred per execution.

Supporters say that if the cost of something is too high, whether it is a phone or murder, then that person will change their behavior towards it, not buying expensive phones and not committing murder.

However, this simple logic, which seems to be engraved into the mind of many ill informed death penalty supporters, does not fully capture the complexity of the issue.

The Views of Experts

Recently, Professor Michael Radelet and Traci Lacock of the University of Colorado completed a study in which they polled the nation's leading criminologists. The researchers found that 88% of those polled do not believe that the death penalty acts as an effective deterrent.

The study was titled "Do Executions Lower Homicide Rates? The Views of Leading Criminologists" and it concluded that "[t]here is [an] overwhelming consensus among America's top criminologists that the empirical research conducted to the deterrence question fails to support the threat or use of the death penalty."

The survey included:

- The Fellows in the American Society of Criminology (ASC)

- Winners of the ASC's Sutherland Award, the highest award given by that organization for contributions to criminological theory.

- Presidents of the ASC between 1997 to present day

Those included in the polls were asked to base their answers on the research available, not their personal opinions on the death penalty.

Here are some of the other statistics that the study found.

- 91% said that politicians only support capital punishment to appear tough on crime

- 75% said that the death penalty distracts legislatures from focusing on real solutions to crime

- 94% agreed that there was little evidence to support the deterrent effect of the death penalty

- 90% said that the death penalty had little effect on overall murder

- 91.6% disagreed with the claim that increasing executions would help deter murders

In another poll, police chiefs were asked to rank factors which they believed reduced crime.

Among the top answers were:

Curbing drug use

More officers

Longer sentences

Gun control

The death penalty consistently ranked last on the lists given.

A Major Boundary For The Death Penalty

There are high costs and risks when the death penalty is involved, so unless it can succeed in saving lives instead of endangering them, there are few, if any, reasons to keep it around. The European Union as well as 101 other countries around the world have concluded that capital punishment is not worth the risks, and they have abolished it. We should follow suit.

A major boundary that must be crossed before the death penalty becomes even remotely deterrent is the cost. The expenses of executing inmates on death row are simply too much to practice on a consistent basis, and thus the chance of a murderer being executed is slim, and is not considered likely in the mind of a murderer.

For example: in California, execution is only the third cause of death of convicts on death row. It sits behind old age and suicide.

Death row supporters say that this can be easily fixed it by speeding up the trials. However, once again this logic is flawed because less appeals means that less of the 68% error rate will be caught, and more of those wrongly convicted will be executed.

Sadly, killing innocent people is an unavoidable cost of the death penalty because of the way the justice system operates. However, if the death penalty cannot save more lives by deterrence than it endangers, it is useless. And currently, there is no evidence of its deterrence.

Death penalty supporters are very quick to point out the few studies that support the deterrence effect. However errors were found in these studies in coding or measuring statistical significance. After these factors were corrected, the studies collapsed.

The studies are riddled with errors, just like the topic they support.

In 2012, The National Academy of Sciences addressed the topic of deterrence head on. They concluded that there was no credible evidence that the death penalty deters homicide, and should thus be removed from discussions of the death penalty.

A Better Way to Deter

Many are not surprised with the conclusion of the National Academy of Sciences. There were 14,000 murders in 2014, but only 35 executions. This creates a 1/400 chance that a murderer will be executed, which isn't enough to discourage anyone who is going to commit murder.

There are better ways to deter crime, such as using the money spent on the death penalty each year to hire new officers.

Over 35 years, California has spent four billion dollars to execute thirteen people. The same amount of money could have been used to train and deploy 80,000 officers, which, if properly assigned, could have prevented 466 murders along with many other forms of crime.

This is a much better deterrent than what even the most optimistic death penalty supporters can hope for with the death penalty.

Simply put: there is no evidence supporting the deterrent factor, but there is a lot of evidence illustrating the high monetary, human, and social costs of capital punishment. The costs simply outweigh the benefits.

"Fundamentally Flawed"

In 2012, The National Research Council concluded that studies claiming that the death penalty affects murder rates are "fundamentally flawed" and used "incomplete or implausible methods."

Murder rates in non-death penalty states have consistently remained lower than the murder rate in death penalty states. The threat of execution at some unforeseen date does not matter to those under the influence of drugs or alcohol, those in a fit of fear or rage, or those with mental illnesses left untreated by the state.

A Useless System

In recent years, five states have abolished the death penalty and more are considering the same course of action. Death penalty supporters claim that this will cause murder rates to rise. However, murder rates are consistently decreasing in direct proportion to the decreasing number of executions. Executions have gone from 98 per annum in 1999 to just 39 in 2013, and the murder rates have fallen from 5.6 per 100,000 people to 4.7 during the same time period.

It is time for the death penalty to receive more criticism. I firmly believe that if the public were more educated about the costs of the death penalty, both monetary and moral, support would steeply decline. There are few reasons to keep the death penalty around. The biggest one has been its alleged deterrent effect. But this assumption must clearly be thrown out, leaving the death penalty almost useless to us as a society. If all it does is take lives, including innocent ones… why is the death penalty still being implemented?

5 MORALITY

In 1890 the U.S. Supreme Court ruled that executions in the U.S. could not include "torture or lingering death." But have we lived up to that standard? Here are the various execution methods currently used in the United States:

Lethal Injection

Lethal Injection was adopted by Oklahoma in 1977. Today all states with the death penalty use it as their main method of execution. The inmate is strapped to a gurney, and needles are inserted into his veins. Long tubes from the needles connect them to several drips.

The first drip is a harmless saline solution, which is administered immediately. Once this happens, the warden signals for the curtain to be raised from in front of a one-way mirror. Behind it are the witnesses for the execution and the families, if they choose to be there.

If the procedure being used is the Three Drug Protocol, the most common form of lethal injection, the inmate is moved to the drip containing sodium thiopental, which puts the inmate to sleep. Next, the tube is moved to a drip containing pancuronium bromide, which paralyzes the inmate. Finally, potassium chloride is administered to stop the inmate's heart.

Professional doctors cannot participate in these executions because it violates their ethical vows. This is often problematic because the injections are left to inexperienced prison staff. If a vein is missed or if the needle becomes clogged, inmates experience extreme pain.

Electrocution

New York built the first electric chair in 1888. It is still used as a secondary method in some states, and thousands have been executed with it since its invention, although some states like Nebraska have ruled it unconstitutional.

The inmate's head and legs are shaved and he is strapped to a chair. A metal cap electrode is attached to his head over a sponge moistened with saline. Another electrode is attached to the inmate's leg, and he is blindfolded.

The executioner pulls a lever, and 500 to 2,000 volts of electricity are released into the inmate's body for about 30 seconds. Doctors wait for the body to cool before checking to see if the inmate is dead. (Doctors are allowed to check if the inmate is dead, but not participate in the electrocution)

If the inmate is still alive, the process is repeated until he is confirmed dead.

During electrocution, the inmate's tissues swell, defecation occurs, steam or smoke rises from their body, and there is a smell of burning.

U.S. Supreme Court Justice William Brennan once offered the following description of an execution by electric chair:

"...the prisoner's eyeballs sometimes pop out and rest on [his] cheeks. The prisoner often defecates, urinates, and vomits blood and drool. The body turns bright red as its temperature rises, and the prisoner's flesh swells and his skin stretches to the point of breaking. Sometimes the prisoner catches fire.... Witnesses hear a loud and sustained sound like bacon frying, and the sickly sweet smell of burning flesh permeates the chamber."

After the inmate is confirmed dead the body is left to cool further before the autopsy begins. According to Robert H. Kirschner, the deputy chief medical examiner of Cook County, "[t]he brain appears cooked in most cases."

The Gas Chamber

The gas chamber was introduced in Nevada in 1924. Gee John was the first to be executed with this method. Five states still use the gas chamber today.

A federal court in California found this method of execution to be cruel and unusual. But when a state's federal court finds an execution method in violation of the 8th amendment, it only applies to that state, so other states are still free to use it.

The gas chamber involves the inmate being strapped to a chair in an airtight chamber and s pail of sulfuric acid is placed below him. When the executioner pulls a lever, sodium cyanide is released into the pail. This causes a chemical reaction that produces fatal doses of cyanide gas.

Inmates are instructed to breath deeply to speed up the process, but many hold their breath and struggle.

According to former warden Clifton Duffy from the San Quenton Penitentiary in California, "At first there is evidence of extreme horror, pain, and strangling. The eyes pop. The skin turns purple and the victim begins to drool."

Dr. Richard Traystman of John Hopkins University School of Medicine says that, "[t]he person is unquestionably experiencing pain and extreme anxiety... The sensation is similar to the pain felt by a person during a heart attack, where essentially the heart is being deprived of oxygen."

Eventually the inmate dies from hypoxia, when oxygen is cut off from the brain.

Firing Squad

Throughout history, the firing squad has rarely been used. The last inmate executed by the firing squad was Ronnie Gardner in 2010.

The inmate is bound to a chair, and sandbags are placed around him to absorb the blood. The inmate is then blindfolded.

Five shooters stand about twenty feet away and aim for the inmate's heart. Four shooters are given bullets and one is given a blank.

On a signal given from the warden, all five fire at the inmate's heart. If the shooters miss, on accident or intentionally, the inmate slowly bleeds out, but if they hit the inmate's heart the process is a bit quicker.

Hanging

Hanging was the primary method of execution used by all states until 1890. Today it is still used in Delaware and Washington.

Before the execution day, the inmate is weighed to determine the "drop" needed to kill them. If the rope is too long compared to their body weight, then the inmate will be decapitated. If it is too short the inmate will slowly strangle to death, which can take up to 45 minutes.

Just before the execution, the inmate is bound and blindfolded. They stand over a trap door, and a noose is placed over their neck.

On a signal, the trapdoor is opened, causing a fracture-dislocation of the neck of the inmate. However, instantaneous death rarely occurs.

According to the Death Penalty Information Center (DPIC):

"If the inmate has strong neck muscles, is very light, if the 'drop' is too short, or the noose has been wrongly positioned, the fracture-dislocation is not rapid and death results from slow asphyxiation. If this occurs the face becomes engorged, the tongue protrudes, the eyes pop, the body defecates, and violent movements of the limbs occur."

Cruel and Unusual Punishment

The history of the death penalty illustrates the American way of using technology to fix any problem. At first there was hanging, which was imported from Britain, and used as the main method of execution during America's early years. The invention of electricity transformed life in the U.S., and transformed the death penalty as well. The result was a new method of execution, the electric chair. Then chemical warfare transformed the death penalty once again, and the gas chamber was instated in Nevada as of 1924.

In 2008, the Chief Justice John Roberts wrote, "the firing squad, hanging, the electric chair, and the gas chamber have each in turn given way to more humane methods, culminating in today's consensus on lethal injection." However, the reality of the situation is far from the simple explanation Justice Roberts suggested.

In 1997, state legislators in Oklahoma asked Jay Chapman to come up with a more *modern* execution method, not a more humane one. Chapman was the state medical examiner, and described himself as "an expert in dead bodies, but not an expert in getting them that way." In spite of this, the state accepted what he came up with: the Three Drug Protocol.

The three drugs to be injected into the inmate were

- sodium thiopental (an anesthetic)

- pancuronium bromide (a paralyzer)

- potassium chloride (a heart stopper)

The Three Drug Protocol was implemented immediately without any tests or studies, and was first used in Texas in 1982. Since then, states have done little to make up for the insufficient research that went into the making of the Protocol. Recently, more and more complications have arisen, and the constitutionality of lethal injection is coming into question.

In 2009, Hospira Inc., the main manufacturer of sodium thiopental, stopped production. Since then, states have been desperately attempting to get their hands on this pain-relieving drug used in executions.

European pharmacies stopped selling it to the U.S. because of pressure from authorities, so states resorted to an uncertified "middle man" in London for their supply. This was until the FDA shut down the operation.

Then they decided to change the protocol, so that sodium thiopental would be replaced with barbiturate pentobarbital. This plan was thwarted when Denmark, the only main manufacturer of the drug, refused to sell it if it was going to be used in executions.

Running out of ideas, many states tried to adopt a One Drug Protocol, using a single overdose of anesthetic to kill inmates.

However, this too had to be abandoned, because doctors protested that the aesthetic being used was necessary in many surgeries, and using it for executions could cause European sources to stop selling the drug to the U.S. completely.

Exhausted of all other sources, the death penalty states decided to rely on "compound pharmacies" to provide the necessary drugs. These pharmacies operate without FDA supervision, and the drugs purchased from them have a high risk of contamination or insufficient effectiveness.

Executions have always been cruel, but now even the most "humane" approach is losing its humanity. The government has moved convicts from the rope to the chamber, and now to the gurney. But the fact remains that we are typing down human beings and killing them. No technology can overcome the injustices that this process entails.

Human Experiments

Nine out of ten executions since the reinstatement of the death penalty in 1976 have been carried out using lethal injection. Yet without properly trained staff members, these operations have gone wrong dozens of times mid-execution, increasingly so since the sodium thiopental shortage.

One such execution was that of Clayton D. Lockett in Oklahoma.

During Lockett's execution, the executioner tried and failed 12 times before he could find a usable vein for delivering the drugs. Finally he found one that he deemed usable in Lockett's groin. After given the sedative and announced unconscious, Lockett began to "speak, buck, raise his head, and writhe against the gurney," according to witnesses at the execution. They also heard him say "[t]his shit is fucking with my mind," "something is wrong," and "the drugs aren't working," as the heart stopping drug was being injected.

Despite this, the execution continued for twenty minutes, (it should usually only take around 10) until the State Director of Corrections declared that Lockett had not received enough drugs to die and that there weren't enough left to continue, so they suspended the execution. Lockett died later that day.

It was clearly a lingering and cruel death.

A new untested drug, midazolam, was used for Lockett's execution. Midazolam is generally used to treat seizures and insomnia, but has no-pain relieving properties.

Lawyers arguing against its use say that, "there is actual scientific and medical data demonstrating that midazolam cannot reliably render a person unconscious and insensate for purposes of undergoing surgery." Nevertheless, Arizona, Florida, and Ohio all used it for executions performed last year.

The lawyers also argue it would be unconstitutional to use a Two Drug Protocol consisting of a paralyzing drug and a heart-stopping drug, because that "would cause intense and needless pain and suffering [which] would be cruel and unusual punishment under the 8th amendment."

There are many means of execution, but the question is if any of them can live up to the standard set by the constitution? If not, then it is obvious that the death penalty has no place in the United States.

The Opinion of Justices

In an article in Time Magazine David Von Drehlc writes:

"In a perfect world, perhaps, the government wouldn't wait 30 years and several hundred executions to determine whether an execution method makes sense. But the world of capital punishment has never been that sort of place. This weighty moral issue, expressive of some of our society's deeply held values, involves a lot of winging it."

Several Justices have publically spoken out against the death penalty.

They include:

- Harry Blackman

He described the endless activity on the death penalty as "tinker[ing] with the machinery of death."

- Sandra Day O'Connor

She told Minnesotans that they should "breathe a big sigh of relief every day" because their state doesn't have the death penalty.

- John Paul Stevens

Stevens voted to restore the death penalty in 1976, but he now speaks of the "serious flaws in the system."

- Lewis F. Powell

A retired Justice, Powell said that if he could change his vote on any one case, he would abolish the death penalty because it "serves no useful purpose," and "brings discredit to the whole legal system."

A Final Word

As the popular saying goes, "We kill people who kill people to show that killing people is wrong." The logic just doesn't add up.

While a murderer has no right to take another's life, it is a problem for society when we so easily take theirs.

6 CLOSURE

This argument has been thrown around so much that I've heard that the families of murder victims call it the "c-word." Once again, the logic is simple, but flawed.

Many think that the families of victims want the guilty party to be executed, and that after seeing these executions the families will find "closure." In reality, many families believe that ending another person's life will not solve anything, and they do not support killing someone in their loved one's name.

There is no one thing that can instantly alleviate the feelings that occur after a traumatic event. But the idea of closure has been so ingrained in to society that many families look to the death penalty in desperation and are bitterly disappointed when they realize that the death penalty offers nothing,

"Horror and Emptiness"

Ronald Carlson wanted revenge against his sister's murderer, but after he witnessed the murderer's execution in 1998 he found a new perspective.

Carlson also said that before his sister's death he had no opinion on capital punishment, but after, he said he "would have killed those responsible with my own hands if given the opportunity." He felt immense and an intense hatred towards her killer.

Carlson went to the execution with the same mindset of most victims' families, but came out a different person. He said:

Watching the execution left me with horror and emptiness, confirming what I had already come to realize: capital punishment only continues the cycle of violence that has a powerful corrosive effect on society." Carlson added that he understands why other families of victims may want the death penalty, but he points out that "[o]ur justice system should not be dictated by vengeance.

And to all death penalty supporters he poses this question: "As a society, shouldn't we be more civilized than the murderers we condemn?"

A Painful System

On March 6, 2015 many family members of victims testified about the exhausting toll the death penalty has taken on their lives. They said that resources wasted on the death penalty could be better used elsewhere.

"I've watched too many families go through this to make me believe this system will ever work," said Kathy Garcia, whose nephew was murdered over 20 years ago.

Most families want the resources to be used for counseling and effective support, rather than committing another murder.

Vicki Schieber, whose daughter was murdered in 1998, said that, "The system is just too painful."

Waiting for Closure

Sandra Millers was looking forward to the execution of her 15-year-old son's murderer for years.

A few days before the execution she said, "I expect to weep tears of joy at seeing him go and tears of sadness for my son. I absolutely want to finalize this pain."

Finally the day came. The day she had been waiting fifteen years for this day to arrive.

But the execution wasn't enough to satisfy her expectations. She was disappointed in it. Miller asked the warden, "Could you give me his body so I could kill him again?"

"I was filled with so much hate," she said. "Then I felt like I knew what it was like to be a killer because I felt like I could be one."

Two years after the execution she has realized that it doesn't bring closure.

"I hate that word," she said. "They should've never invented it."

Miller told the press that during those fifteen years of waiting for "closure," she became an alcoholic, had two heart attacks, became depressed, and attempted suicide on multiple occasions.

Many families experience this; waiting for the day that is supposed to heal them, only realizing that all it does is leave them disappointed and empty.

Pat Bane, former president of Murder Victims' Families for Reconciliation, points out, "[y]ou spend ten years hating someone, then you wake up the next morning, and he's dead. What do you do with that hatred? They haven't healed it because that grief has been put on hold waiting for some magic bullet to end it all."

But that bullet will never come through the killing of another person. In fact, a magic bullet will never come at all. But gradually, with counseling and the right resources, it is possible to heal.

A Rare Study

Studies addressing this very topic are rare, with statistics and money dominating the content of most scientific studies. However, there is one study by two researchers, one from the University of Texas, and the other from the University of Minnesota, addressing this topic.

Texas executes more inmates than any other state, and is

responsible for about 1/3 of all executions in the U.S. each year.

Minnesota, on the other hand, does not practice the death penalty, and therefore executes zero people each year.

This study reports from a neutral perspective. The researchers have said that the study is neither in support nor opposition of the death penalty. The study concluded that it is flawed to assume that the death penalty brings satisfaction or closure to the victim's families.

The researchers come to this conclusion by interviewing families of murder victims in both states. They found that the victim's families in Minnesota have better physical, psychological, and behavioral health as well as a higher satisfaction with the justice system than the families from Texas.

Umbriet, the lead author, said: "You could say that, if you really are concerned about the healing impact of the ultimate penal sanction on family survivors, there's a clear indication that the death penalty doesn't foster that in the long term."

While the deterrence of the death penalty has been disproven, it has now also been proven that there have been innocent people on death row, and now even the accepted fact of closure to families has been challenged.

No One-Size-Fits-All Solution

The government and prosecutors have always assumed that executions bring closure to families. But considering all the data available, it is clear that there is no one-size-fits-all method to bring "closure."

Law professor Lynne Henderson says that the needs of every family differs, as do their responses to the tragedy. After talking to many victims' families, Henderson said, "common assumptions about crime victims — that they are all 'outraged' and want revenge and tougher law enforcement — underline much of the current victim's rights rhetoric. But in light of the existing psychological evidence, these assumptions fail to address the experience and real needs of past victims."

Often the trials and execution simply provide an outlet for pointing the finger, and then fuel the rage.

Many crime victims report that endlessly repeating their tragic stories during years of appeals increases stress and delays the healing process rather than giving "closure."

This doesn't mean that some families don't want the execution of the murderer. But they often want it for the wrong reasons, or because of the fact that the government has assured them that closure will be a result. There is no such thing as closure when someone dear to you has been taken from you.

"The Death Penalty Paradox"

In an article I recently read, Margery Eagan discussed "The Death Penalty Paradox."

This is what she said:

"The execution [families of victims] want can turn out not to ease their grief but keep them wrapped up, entwined, even entrapped by the minute particulars of the killer's life — and fate."

Executions divide a family when they need each other most. They are separated into those who want the death penalty and those who don't. This delays a family's ability to put the killer out of their mind, and ultimately, to heal.

The death penalty is about revenge and hate, but keeping those emotions fresh for years of appeals damages the healing process more than it helps.

The Myth

For hundreds upon hundreds of families, another murder gives them no "closure."

To them, closure is a myth — something that it always dangled in front of them, but they can never reach. The death penalty is a spotlight for the defendants and the prosecutors at the expense of the victims and their families.

Every time an execution takes place, you can be sure that the families of the victims were not magically healed, but only made to suffer longer.

7 THE COST

It can often be hard to relate to how a murderer feels before he kills, or what its like when a family loses a member. But there is something that we can all relate to, the financial cost of the death penalty. This affects all of us, whether you realize it or not, because the death penalty is paid for by raising taxes and taking away funding from highways and police. These are your tax dollars at work; make sure that they are used well.

Simply More Expensive

Simply put, the death penalty costs more than life without parole. Many of those who support the Death Penalty do not realize this; once again simple but false logic is their downfall. They think, "well, I don't want my tax dollars spent covering the costs of keeping a murderer alive." And while they are correct that if a convict gets punished with life without parole tax dollars will be spent on them until they die, the amount spent on them during that period is nothing compared to how much it costs for a capital case.

This is mainly because the Constitution requires a long and complicated judicial process for capital cases in an attempt to prevent innocent lives from being taken. But we both know how good they are at that...

Despite this, less appeals would mean less innocent people would be exonerated, and even more of those wrongly convicted would perish.

If life without parole were the maximum punishment it would save each individual death penalty state millions of dollars each year. This money could be spent on things that actually benefit society such as:

-Education

-Roads

-Police Recruitment and Training

-Public Safety Programs

-Drug and Alcohol Treatment

-Child Abuse Protection Programs

-Mental Health Services

-Services for victims of crime and their families

For example, California could save $1 billion after just five years of replacing the Death Penalty program with permanent imprisonment as the maximum punishment. Taxpayers in California pay $90,000 more to house each death row inmate verses keeping them in a high security prison. And as I have said, execution in California is only the third leading cause of death on death row.

It is estimated that costs for California will reach $9 billion by 2030, and the current costs are $137 million a year. Costs where the maximum punishment is Life Without Parole would be just $1.5 million.

The 5 Reasons for the Rising Cost

The costs of the Death Penalty have been studied carefully in many states including:

-California

-Colorado

-Florida

-Idaho

-Indiana

-Kansas

-Maryland

-Nevada

-New Jersey

-New York

-North Carolina

-Oregon

-Tennessee

-Texas

-Washington

In all of these states the cost of the Death Penalty is on the rise.

A report in 2010 found that between 1989 and 1997 the median cost of a capital case that went to trial was $269,139. The same study found that between 1998 and 2004 that cost had risen to $620,932.

There are 5 main reasons for the rapidly rising prices of capital cases.

1. Attorney Pay

Lawyers spend more time preparing for capital cases than any other case because of the high stakes and the complexity. Prosecutors are not paid by the hour but they do employ staff that are paid hourly to help research the case.

Between 1989 and 1997, attorneys spent an average of 1,889

hours preparing for trial. Between 1998 and 2004 the time spent pre-trial had risen to 3,557.

The defense team is usually court appointed, and they are paid by the hour. Most counties pay their defense lawyers at least $100 an hour. This includes pre-trial preparation.

2. Experts

In capital cases experts are becoming more and more necessary to both sides. An example of this is a simple psychiatric evaluation of the defendant.

Before, an IQ test and a simple interview would be all you needed. But now psychiatrists compile a complete Mental Health History of the defendant.

"Experts may also be needed to explain why mistaken eyewitness identification commonly occurs, or to explain why someone might falsely confess," says Natasha Minsker, Associate Director of the American Civil Liberties Union of Northern California. In a 2008 report she also said, "Modern Science has greatly enhanced our ability to distinguish the innocent from the guilty… but it all costs money."

Defense lawyers and prosecutors are constantly competing for the best expert.

"I won't use anybody to do autopsies except for triple bond certified forensic pathologists," says Randal Sims, District Attorney of Potter County in Texas, "so that I don't wind up having one only certified in one area, and then the defense has a better one."

3. Unpredictability

Steadily, the standards regarding what needs to occur in order for a capital case to be considered constitutional are rising. And with this rise come new and more expensive legal battles.

An example of this is the case of Brittany Holberg. It is estimated that the prosecution paid between $500,000 and $700,000 to get the death penalty. Then during the appeals new defense lawyers found reason to believe that Holberg didn't have a fair trial.

They appealed and prosecutors had to pay $300,000 more 2011-2014 just to keep the death sentence.

A death sentence can be overturned for multiple reasons, whether it is the fault of a defense lawyer, prosecutor, a single incorrect instruction given to the jury, or a single piece of evidence that was not shown.

If any of these conditions are met a new trial occurs, and with it more appeals, and overall more money.

4. The Jury

In 2011, United States 9th Circuit Court Judge Arther L. Alarcon and attorney Paula Michell published a massive study on the costs of the Death Penalty.

They found that jury selection for Capital Cases take a month longer than usual murder cases and cost about $200,000 more on average.

This is because as support for the Death Penalty falls, it becomes harder and harder to find 12 jurors who are willing to execute if necessary. This means more hours for attorneys, judges, and court staff, ultimately costing more and more money.

5. Death Row

Death row inmates are always housed in solitary confinement, which also costs more.

As appeals become longer and executions slow down, these costs quickly add up.

This is most apparent in California, which has the largest death row population, but rarely executes. The yearly cost of housing and medical bills for death row inmates in California is $184 million.

Death Penalty supporters have always argued that your tax dollars should not be wasted on paying the medical bills of the old, however this is now happening anyways.

A Price Tag

If you had to put a price on the Death Penalty it would be about $90 million a year. This is how much California would save if it abolished the Death Penalty.

I have heard Death Penalty supporters argue that you cannot put a price on justice. But the truth is, cost does matter when making decisions about public policy.

Does the death penalty provide more justice than Life Without Parole? Even if it does, is this strain of justice worth $90 million a year?

Quotes about Cost of The Death Penalty

Sterling Goodspeed, former district attorney of Warren County, New York:

I think I could prove to you that I could put someone in the Waldorf Hotel for 60 to 70 years and feed them three meals a day cheaper than we can litigate a single Death Penalty case.

Kansa State Senator, Carolyn McGinn:

We've had the Death Penalty… and we continue to pay for the process with little results… But we continue to cut the programs that could prevent these types of crimes.

James Abbott, Police Chief of West Orange, New Jersey:

As a police chief, I find this use of state resources offensive… Give a law enforcement professional like me $250 million, and I'll show you how to reduce crime. The Death Penalty isn't anywhere on my list.

8 ULTIMATE JUSTICE

Death penalty supporters say that those who kill deserve to die. Anything less would be undervaluing the victim's life, they argue.

In my opinion it is barbaric and primitive to use the "eye for an eye" excuse for the death penalty. Let's rape rapists and steal from thieves as well then; same logic, right?

As Gandhi says, "An eye for an eye will leave the whole world blind."

Before you make a decision on your stance on the death penalty, I will ask you one question:

Although you'd be correct in saying that a murderer had no right to take a life, but what gives *you* the right to take theirs?

9 CONCLUSION

You have read what I have to say, and now you are no longer part of the ill informed masses. Whether you agree with me or not is up to you, what you do with the information is up to you, and whether you pass on the information is up to you.

The death penalty has been plaguing our society for decades, and I did something about it — I wrote a book. What will you do?

Books, offers, and more at

liamwallbooks.com

ABOUT THE AUTHOR

Liam Wall grew up in Ireland, but currently lives in California. When he is not writing he is performing magic for whoever will 'pick a card.'

Printed in Great Britain
by Amazon